For Derek

"I'm a BIG FAN of My Boyfriend. The Romance & Fun Quiz Book for Couples, Year 1: The Romantic Gift for Boyfriend or A Couple Playing Together to Cherish Memories of Their Love's First year!"
Series: BIG FAN Quizzes & Questions Book Vol.1

By Octavia O. Hart

ISBN-10 : 1537468316
ISBN-13 : 978-1537468310

User's manual

1. This book comes with 5 sets of quizzes, and each set of quizzes comes with 20 questions. Each question carries 1 mark.

2. You can start with any set of quizzes, and can play either all sets in one go, or one by one.

3. After finishing a set of quizzes, give the book to your loved one for the corrected answers and the score summary.

4. Be awarded a coupon if you pass the pass mark set by your loved one!

5. If you didn't win a coupon, don't lose hope! There is still a bonus coupon that comes with THE last question bonus!

6. Enjoy using your coupons and keep those precious memories in the extra scrap pages at the back of the book!

"I'm a BIG FAN of My Boyfriend" comes with its equal, "I'm a BIG FAN of My Girlfriend", also available on online & brick-and-mortar book stores.

You can either play one of the two books, or play them both together by exchanging the books between you and your loved one. In latter case, some creative fun can be added e.g. to be merciful to your other half by giving hints to questions, compete - instead of using the pass mark – so only the winner would get the coupon, or to decide together what to write on the coupons prior to the start of the games. Possibilities are limitless.

● ● ●

Vow

"We do solemnly swear…
To play fair, love, laugh, and learn.
Answer honestly, and follow through
with promised rewards"

(signed)

Table of Contents

Between You & Me

1

Among the gifts I've given him,

Lego figures ....

is the one my boyfriend likes
the most.

Score $\bar{0}$

Between You & Me

2

I'm positive that
my boyfriend thinks
I look drop dead gorgeous
when I wear

.... anything low cut! ....

Score 1

Between You & Me

3

You know what!
My boyfriend is confident that

........*his chest !*........

is the sexiest part of his body.

Score ⟨O⟩

Between You & Me

4

Good at art?

is my positive character that
my boyfriend always tells his
friends about.

Score | 1

Between You & Me

5

When..........*his*..........*feeling*..........

..........*low*..........

is a situation when my boyfriend
wants me to be with him most.

Score 0

Between You & Me

6

Between

A morning kiss
&
A goodnight kiss,

my boyfriend thinks that

............*a goodnight kis*............

is the more romantic one.

Score | |

Between You & Me

7

My boyfriend's shoe size is

6-8

Score 1

Between You & Me

8

My boyfriend is a

a. Back sleeper

b. Side sleeper

c. Stomach sleeper

d. He never sleeps

Score ½

Between You & Me

9

My boyfriend's usual
sleeping hours is

from....*1:30*....to....*7:30*....

Score 1

10

I won't let anyone tease my
boyfriend about

..........*his hairier ?*..........;
he's quite sensitive about it.

Score $\frac{1}{2}$

Between You & Me

11

Whenever he feels nervous,
my boyfriend would

.... *tune things slowly* ....
to remain calm.

Score 1

Between You & Me

12

It's

 True   False

that my boyfriend has a scar on his body because of an accident during his childhood.

Score

Between You & Me

13

My boyfriend

☑ Can   ☐ Can't

sing!

Score

14

My boyfriend is a

☐ Good   ☑ Bad

dancer!

Score 1

Between You & Me

15

The most ticklish spot on my boyfriend's body is

..............his   feet..............

Score 1

Between You & Me

16

At his best ability, my boyfriend can get himself ready to go to work

within ...*30*... minutes after waking up.

Score 1

Between You & Me

17

The prtlheal

uees of the INPI

is one of my boyfriend's
pet peeves.

Score 1

Between You & Me

18

.... *smiles* ! ....

is the first thing my boyfriend does
in the bathroom every day.

Score ◯

Between You & Me

19

My boyfriend usually goes to bed

with ☐ *1* pieces of cloth.

Score ☐ *0*

Between You & Me

20

My boyfriend is allergic to

...........*hay!*...................

Score 0

Between You & Me

This coupon entitles you to:

Redeemable : ....

Expiration date : ....

Sum Score

I'm a Mind Reader

1

If he is to pick ONLY one, my boyfriend would definitely go for a

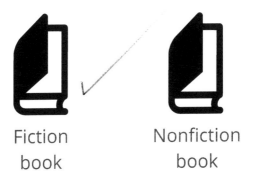

Fiction
book

Nonfiction
book

Score

I'm a Mind Reader

2

I have many interests,
but my interest in

................_languages_................

is what impresses my boyfriend
most.

Score

I'm a Mind Reader

3

My boyfriend would agree with me
that it will be so much fun
if we are to

go to New Zealand!!

together, and that we should try it
at least once!

Score

I'm a Mind Reader

4

Coffee or Tea?

My boyfriend goes for

~~Hot choc~~

more often.

Score

I'm a Mind Reader

5

When it comes to cooking,
the one dish my boyfriend
thinks he can do best is

......*sandwiches!*......

Score

I'm a Mind Reader

6

A card or a cake.
If he could only have one,
my boyfriend would want a

c a k e

for his birthday.

34

I'm a Mind Reader

7

I know what my boyfriend would choose, between

&

A cat

A dog

Score

I'm a Mind Reader

Between
a Concert and a Magic show;
my boyfriend prefers going to a

Concert

Score

I'm a Mind Reader

9

My boyfriend knows that I like

.....Watch Easterles..... so much,
so he always does it with me
although he doesn't like it as much.
That's very thoughtful of him!

Score

I'm a Mind Reader

10

'

....

is the place my boyfriend thinks
it would be great if I join him and
his friends sometimes.

Score

I'm a Mind Reader

11

....

is one thing my boyfriend would like to remind me about, because he cares so much about me.

Score

I'm a Mind Reader

12

If he had a chance to make one wish that will definitely become true, my boyfriend would definitely wish for us to

....

Score

I'm a Mind Reader

13

…..is a friend of my boyfriend's whom he shares most secrets with.

Score

I'm a Mind Reader

14

When my boyfriend becomes
unusually quiet, I know that he

....

Score

I'm a Mind Reader

15

....

is the budget my boyfriend would take me out for our most important dinner of this year.

I'm a Mind Reader

16

If possible, my boyfriend would prefer a house

☐ by the lake   ☐ by the sea

Score ☐

I'm a Mind Reader

17

....

is the sports my boyfriend believes
he is best at.

Score

I'm a Mind Reader

18

Rich or Famous?

.

.

My boyfriend would rather be

.... than ....

Score

I'm a Mind Reader

19   Imagining that we could live
100 years from now...,
in my boyfriend's head, the picture
of him and I would look like this

Draw it here ➜

Score

I'm a Mind Reader

20

My boyfriend

☐ Does   ☐ Does not

agree with the statement
"Money can't buy happiness".

Score ☐

I'm a Mind Reader

This coupon entitles you to:

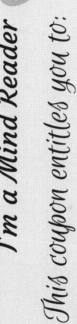

Redeemable : ....

Expiration date : ....

Sum Score

Mad About

1

....

is one of those Hollywood flicks
my boyfriend would pick to watch
at home on a rainy Sunday
afternoon.

Score

Mad About

2

I know for sure.

.... is my
boyfriend's most favorite color.

Score

Mad About

3

My boyfriend's most favorite
room of the house is

....

Score ☐

Mad About

4

....

is a kind of food my boyfriend
never tastes and would love to try.

Score

Mad About

5

My boyfriend would definitely not reject a night out with me at

....

Score

Mad About

6

I know my boyfriend would LOVE
to have a car that looks like this…

Draw it here

Score

Mad About

7

Winter, Spring, Summer, or Fall...

My boyfriend's most favorite
season is

....

Score

Mad About

8

....

is one thing that could make my
boyfriend stay up all night.

Score

Mad About

9 Here's my boyfriend's most favorite type of mens underwear.

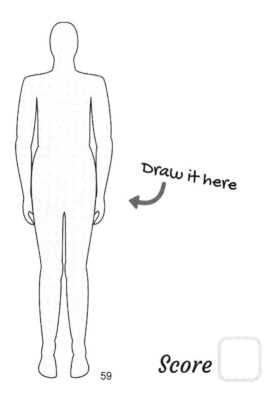

Draw it here

Score

Mad About

10 I can pick an ice-cream flavor for my boyfriend that he would surely enjoy; and that flavor is

....

Score

Mad About

11

My boyfriend can do this all day

....

Score

Mad About

12

....

is a famous person my boyfriend
would love to talk to over a cup
of coffee.

Score

Mad About

13

....
is one of my boyfriend's
favorite pastimes.

Score

Mad About

14

My boyfriend thinks

....

is one of the greatest movies
ever made.

Score

Mad About

15

My boyfriend likes
the songs of this artist

....

Score

Mad About

16

Apart from Happy Birthday and the national anthem,

....

is one of the contemporary songs my boyfriend can sing along really well.

Score

Mad About

17

write it here

is one of my boyfriend's
favorite TV shows.

Score

Mad About

18

I know if I plan our next trip to

....,

my boyfriend would be so
happy that he would surely
jump with joy.

Score

Mad About

19

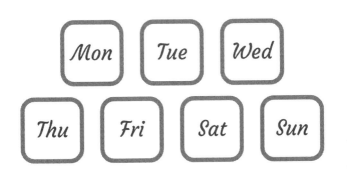

Mon	Tue	Wed

Thu	Fri	Sat	Sun

is his most favorite day
of the week.

Score

Mad About

20

My boyfriend thinks that

. . . .

is one of the most inspirational
men alive.

Score

Mad About

This coupon entitles you to:

Redeemable : ....

Expiration date : ....

Sum Score

Rekindle Old Memories

1 Among the pictures that we happily took together, the one that is my boyfriend's most favorite is this one..

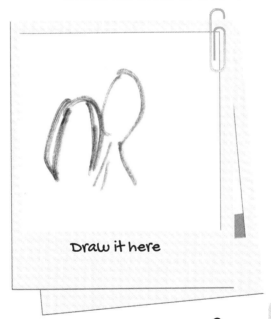

Draw it here

Score

2

........*English* ✓........

is the subject my boyfriend
loved the most in school.

Score

Rekindle Old Memories

3

Among the places
we have been together,

Iceland

....

is one of my boyfriend's most
favorite spots.

Score

Rekindle Old Memories

4 A nickname my boyfriend was called by his close friends when he was younger is

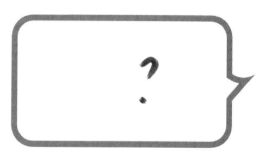

Score

Rekindle Old Memories

5

My boyfriend believes that
he and I meet each other by

 Chance  Choice

Score

Rekindle Old Memories

6

What my boyfriend loves the
most about our first date was

Seeing boobs on stage
jk!

Score

Rekindle Old Memories

7

Back on the very first day we met,
my boyfriend's impression
of me was that

I was chatty + fun

Score

Rekindle Old Memories

8

When my boyfriend was a child,
he wanted to be

....

Isn't he adorable!

Score

Rekindle Old Memories

9

Penicuik

....

is my boyfriend's hometown.

Score

Rekindle Old Memories

10

When my boyfriend was a kid,

.... was the snack he loved.

Score

Rekindle Old Memories

11

When my boyfriend was a child, one of his most favorite toys was

....

Score

Rekindle Old Memories

12

I know that the location of
our first date

□ is   □ is not

my boyfriend's 100% own idea.

Score □

Rekindle Old Memories

13

My boyfriend thinks that

☐ I   ☐ he

was the one who made
the first move.

Score ☐

Rekindle Old Memories

My boyfriend had his first crush

when he was ⬜ years old.

Score ⬜

Rekindle Old Memories

15

The name of my boyfriend's
elementary school is

....

Score

Rekindle Old Memories

16 It is

[ ] True

[ ] False

that my boyfriend had at least one imaginary friend when he was a child.

Score [ ]

Rekindle Old Memories

17 Here is what my boyfriend would sum up what he has learned about life, in three words.

....

....

....

Score

Rekindle Old Memories

18

One thing my boyfriend has dreamed of since he was a child, and it has not yet been realized is

....

Score

Rekindle Old Memories

19

....

is what he thought about my
look on our first date.

Score

Rekindle Old Memories

20

Since the day we became a boyfriend and a girlfriend, there is one thing my boyfriend has always wanted to tell me but he didn't tell me yet; that is

· ·

· ·

· ·

Score

Rekindle Old Memories

This coupon entitles you to:

Redeemable : ....
Expiration date : ....

Sum Score

That's SO you!

1 If he were a screenwriter, assigned to rescript the ending of Romeo & Juliet, I'm pretty sure my boyfriend would rewrite it to be

write it here

Score

That's SO you!

2

If a party was themed

....,
my boyfriend will be dying to
go for that party.

Score

That's SO you!

3

....

is a kind of food that my
boyfriend will never EVER eat!

Score ☐

That's SO you!

4

My boyfriend would be so pleased if people would describe him, in one word, as

...........lovable...........

Score ☐

That's SO you!

5

My boyfriend would have no problem going to a museum of

.............Lego.............

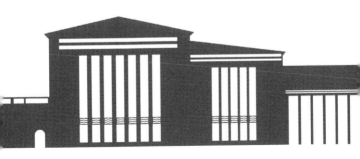

Score ☐

That's SO you!

6

If today is the day he has to leave for a mission to mars, what my boyfriend would say to me would be

"

I love you. You are strong. I'll be back before you know it!

"

Score

That's SO you!

7

If he happened to win a one million dollar prize, my boyfriend would definitely spend some, if not all, of it on

 LEGO

Score

That's SO you!

8

My boyfriend would say that

...............writing...............

is his talent he is most proud of.

Score

That's SO you!

9 If my boyfriend were a superhero, he would want to have this superpower

invisibility

Score

That's SO you!

10

Joking about

.... *nothing!* ......

is what my boyfriend thinks
it is ALWAYS a bad joke.

Score

That's SO you!

11

The first new year resolution that my boyfriend broke this year was

....

Score

That's SO you!

12

If my boyfriend were a spy,
he would have loved to be
nicknamed

" _____Deadly D_____ "

Score

That's SO you!

13

Shhh…, my boyfriend is scared of this animal

 draw it here

Score

That's SO you!

14

arrogant show off nerds
....

is a type of person that my
boyfriend dislikes the most.

Score

That's SO you!

15

My boyfriend could imagine taking me out to dinner in outer space,

on our year anniversary.

Score

That's SO you!

16

I'm sure my boyfriend
would be overjoyed if I say
this to him

"

...... You're the best ......

...... guy I've known ......

"

Score

That's SO you!

17

I am so sure my boyfriend

[ ] does [✓] does not

know what the word
"defenestration"
means.

Score [ ]

That's SO you!

18

I'm sure that my boyfriend

 does ☐ does not

know which one, between
Schadenfreude and Arzerbaijan,
is the name of a country.

Score ☐

That's SO you!

19

Without doubt,

Changing Sheets

is the household chore my
boyfriend hates the most.

Score

That's SO you!

20 If we were invited to a most luxurious party, my boyfriend would feel most comfortable in this attire.

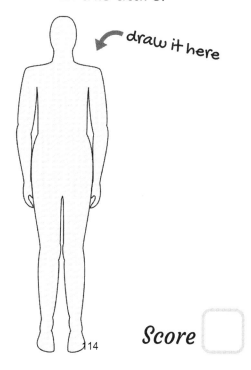

draw it here

Score

That's SO you!

This coupon entitles you to:

Redeemable : ....

Expiration date : ....

Sum Score

Bonus

My boyfriend :

> Write me a message telling me why you should get this bonus coupon.

Me :

> ....
> ....
> ....
> ....*(continue on next page)*

Bonus

Me :

....

....

....

....

....

....

....

Score

Bonus

This coupon entitles you to:

Redeemable : ....

Expiration date : ....

Sum Score

precious moments

precious moments

Other books by Octavia O. Hart & Lots of Love Publishing

Valentine's Day
Kids Coloring Book

You & Me :
The Journal While
We Are Apart

Me & You :
The Journal While
We Are Apart

*Available now on online &
brick-and-mortar bookstores.*